Brian Palmer

Football Referees ?
You must be joking !

2nd Edition 2015

Author's Note

Maybe surprisingly, referees actually love refereeing, usually because they enjoy or have enjoyed playing, and want to stay involved by enabling others to enjoy the game.

So, where does the humour come in?

Well, as we all know, there is humour as well as drama in many football situations, and funnies about referees abound. The truth is that referees enjoy them too, tell them to each other as well as to players and fans. We are not embarrassed to be thought at least half-mad, blind and of doubtful parentage . .
This collection of jokes, quotations, wise sayings, limericks, anecdotes and so on, represents a good variety, though inevitably, some major themes come through. Fortunately, football pundits and managers as well as players and referees continue to provide some hilarious stories, lines and gaffes – long may they go on – and the refereeing community sporadically adds to its own store of jokes. This particular collection, however, contains much original material too in all the categories.

Go on, don't be embarrassed, have a laugh on us !

Last time the referee gave us
a penalty away from home,
Christ was still a carpenter.

Lenny Lawrence

Warhurst was sent off for foul
and abusive language, but the
lad swears blind he never
spoke to the linesman.

Joe Royle

The referee in charge of a local derby was having almost every decision questioned. When he had to send two players off for fighting he called the captains together to tell them to calm everything down.

Just then, a dog ran on to the pitch. Quick as a flash one of the players shouted:

"OK lads. The game should improve now - the ref's guide dog's arrived."

Have you heard the one about the referee who paid to see a mind reader?

She gave him his money back.

You don't have to be mad to be a referee – but it certainly helps.

One of Gary Linekar's sons was doing his homework. "Dad, what's a masochist?"

Gary: "Someone who gets pleasure from suffering pain".

Son: "That's no good Dad. It has to be only one word.

Gary: "Referee?"

Reluctantly the instructor had to reject the applicant for the referee training course.

He discovered that the young man could name both his parents, had perfect eyesight and did not indulge in self-abuse.

A top Russian official, Alexei Spirin, was suspended after having awarded a penalty against Dynamo Moscow – after two of their own players collided.

Extract from the referee's report on a player yellow-carded for diving:

"I cautioned him for descent."

The referee went to his doctor with real earache, not the sort habitually given to him by the players and fans. When the doctor heard the problem described, he took out his otoscope and inserted the end into his patient's ear. After only a moment, he withdrew the instrument and said: "Excuse me, sir, are you by any chance a football referee?"

"As it happens I am," the patient replied. "Why do you ask?"

"I thought you must be. It's just that I can see right through to the other side."

Man who cannot see what all other people see, he football referee.

Man who can make eleven bosom friends and eleven sworn enemies with single word, like 'penalty', he football referee.

Referee trainer: "How did you find the candidates from our recent training course?"

Referee examiner: "Quite good in general but one was a bit of a worry. When I asked him to tell me about a dropped ball, he said he hadn't been told anything about first aid."

Wife: "Refereeing, Football, Refereeing, Football, Refereeing. You never think of anything else. If you said one weekend you were going to stay at home and help me in the house, I'd drop dead from shock."

Referee husband: "Now you're trying to tempt me."

Soccer referees, it would appear, are a disappointing breed. The Football League say that fewer and fewer referees are applying to join the League panel . . . and I can't say I'm surprised. After all, there can't be that many deaf, blind and stupid illegitimate children born in a country the size of England.

Paul Hince

At the beginning of the training course the trainee referee had been given a copy of the LOAF – the 17 Laws of Association Football. During the course his instructors frequently referred to Law 18 – *common sense.*

At the final session, the senior instructor asked for any questions and saw that one of the trainees was looking puzzled and anxious. "Have you a problem?"

"Yes. I've kept on looking but I can't find Law 18 anywhere in *my* book."

It was a local league match and the referee called the captains together for the start of the game. They shook hands but, when he felt in his pocket for his coin, the referee realised he had left it in the changing room. Thinking quickly, he produced his whistle, showed it to the two captains, put his hands behind his back and then extended two fists towards them.

"Your call, Blues"

"Heads."

Of course referees are inconsistent. They give a lot more penalties to them than they give to us.

A referee who goes to see a psychiatrist ought to have his head examined.

The football fan walks into a souvenir shop in Hamelin, home of the legendary Pied Piper, while on holiday in Germany, and his eye is caught by an ornamental brass rat. He thinks "That'll be perfect for my mother-in-law's birthday", so he asks the shopkeeper how much it is. "€20 for the rat and €200 for the story", replies the shopkeeper. "No story", says the tourist, and hands over a €20 note.

As he is walking away from the shop, he realises a live rat has appeared and is following him at a discreet distance. Then another, and another, and soon there is a squeaking procession behind him. He's terrified but fortunately he's arrived at a bridge over the famous River Weser. Without a moment's hesitation, he throws the brass rat into the waters below. To his astonishment all the other rats leap into the water like lemmings.

The man quickly makes his way back to the shop.

"I thought you'd be back", the shopkeeper says knowingly. "I suppose you want to invest €200 in the story now".

"No way" says the man. "I just wondered if you had any brass referees . . . ."

I know where he should have put his flag up, and he'd have got plenty of help

Ron Atkinson

If he fouls you, he normally picks you up, but the referee doesn't see what he picks you up by.

Ryan Giggs on Denis Wise

One day, while the seven dwarfs were deep in the mine, there was a rock fall. When they didn't arrive home at the usual time, Snow White went to see what was wrong. She called anxiously down the mine and was greeted by a faint response:

"I want to be a referee; I want to be a referee".

Snow White smiled in relief: "Well at least Dopey's still alive."

"It takes some believing for a referee to mix up two players as different in appearance as we are. I'm 5ft 8in and white, and he's about 6ft 4in and black."

Tony Spearing of Plymouth,
after the referee cautioned him
and not Tony Witter, the real offender,
against Leicester.

When red and yellow cards were first introduced, it is reported, a well-known referee had to deal with cautionable misconduct by two players. He took out his yellow card, showed it to each of them, then proceeded solemnly to tear it in two and gave them half each.

"Dad. Why do most referees wear black?"

"Because they're going to a funeral, son."

"Whose funeral are they going to, Dad?"

"Theirs"

Arsène Wenger was having trouble sleeping. He went to the doctor who sent him on to a consultant psychiatrist.

The psychiatrist asked Arsène to describe the problem briefly.

"I get to sleep quickly enough but I wake up in the middle of the night in a cold sweat thinking I am a referee"

"Aha," purred the psychiatrist knowingly.

"Oh no, that's not the only problem," Arsène added quickly. "I suddenly realise that one of the teams is Arsenal and they've fouled in the penalty area."

After the referee had had a nightmare of a match, the assessor, ever mindful of his responsibility, chose his words carefully :

"On the basis of your performance today I don't really think you should be refereeing at this level."

Deeply concerned, the referee related what had happened to his friend, the senior assistant, who was quick to console him.

"Don't take it too much to heart, mate. He doesn't know what he's talking about. He only repeats what everybody else is saying."

Ten inmates
of Parkhurst Prison,
Isle of Wight,
have qualified as referees.

They have the distinct
advantage of knowing a lot
about not obeying Laws.

Conversation overheard in the pub after a game one Sunday morning:

First player: "What's the difference between God and a referee?"

Second Player: "I don't know. What *is* the difference between God and a referee?"

First player: "God doesn't think he's a referee!"

After the final whistle of the international match, one of the captains went up to the English referee, shook his hand and said:

"Thank you, referee. We always like it when we have English officials because they are so fair."

The referee beamed with pleasure.

"You get it wrong for *both* teams!"

What's the difference between an aeroplane kit and a referee?

One is a glueless kit, the other is a clueless git.

The referee and his two assistants were walking towards the officials' entrance at the Football League ground, when a funeral cortège approached along the adjacent road. The referee paused, turned towards the hearse and stood motionless, head bowed. His assistants thought they'd better do likewise. When the procession had passed, one of them remarked:

"That was really nice. It's not often people show such respect nowadays."

"Well, I had been married to her for 15 years", responded the referee.

Joe Kinnear landed in hot water yet again for criticising a referee.

"I couldn't believe it when the ref gave the decision to the opposition," he moaned.

Video evidence later confirmed, however, that the opposing captain had indeed correctly called 'heads'.

At the end of the day, refereeing means you don't have to spend your Saturdays at Sainsbury's.

The young shop assistant asked his boss whether he could have Saturday afternoon off to attend his uncle's funeral. The boss, a keen football fan, was suspicious because there was a local derby cup-tie on the Saturday. However, he decided to trust the lad and gave his permission.

As the boss was going to his seat at the game, he passed his employee on the steps. "I thought you told me you wanted the afternoon off to go to your uncle's funeral."

"It was true sir. He's the referee . . ."

"Why should referees be kept
  300ft under ground?"

"I don't know. Why *should*
referees be kept 300ft under
ground?"

"Because deep down they are
very nice people."

The innovative Cybernetics and Robotics Department of the famous university came up with the brilliant idea of a football referee robot. They were convinced that the technology was now ready for the break-through. However, development costs would be high, so the university needed reassurance that the product would sell.

The Marketing Department of the Business School would carry out a survey of football administrators, club management, coaches, players, fans and, of course, the media.

The plans were quietly shelved when the unanimous response was that 'not having a referee to abuse would destroy the enjoyment of the game' !

I suppose that he was at least consistent. He was bad all night.

George Graham

It was like the referee had a new yellow card and wanted to see if it worked.

Richard Rufus

The young (male) referee had been given a senior girl's game for the first time.

After the disappointment at not being allowed to share the teams' changing room, all went well. The players were skilful and honest – no niggling fouls, no simulation, no problems. Then, late in the game, a nasty clash of heads between an attacker and a defender.

The attacker went down as if pole-axed. The referee, mindful of his elementary first aid sprinted to her side. He checked straightaway that she was breathing, but her breathing was worryingly shallow. Firmly he said into her ear:

"Big breaths."

To his relief, her eyes opened and a smile spread slowly across her face. "Yeth, I know. And I'm only thicthteen"

Referee: "Number 7.
        I'm sending you off."

Player: "What for ref?"

Referee: "For the rest of
        the match of course!"

When the local Sunday League manager saw the referee approaching before the match, he said confidentially to the captain:

"Be careful. This is the one with the inflated ego."

The captain replied in all seriousness: "I know. I think he's that shape because he likes a Guinness or two after the game."

Assessor : That was a
really good game today

The referee beamed

Pity you seemed to miss
most of it !

It was Rangers v Celtic and the two managers visited the referee in his changing room to deliver their team sheets and get any final instructions. The referee was satisfied and said: "Well, I think that's everything then".

"Not quite", said one of the managers," Could we just have the name and address of your next-of-kin".

The referee raised his arm to signal the indirect free kick. Instant shout from the crowd :

"Sure you *can* leave the ground - and the sooner, the better " !

The referee instructor had carefully explained to his trainees the importance of using the whistle properly.

After a practical training session he took one of his charges to one side and quietly but firmly reminded him about the need to blow the whistle properly – it needed to *talk.*

"Well, I tried" protested the trainee. "But it's no use just telling me - you ought to tell the bloody whistle."

An Assistant Referee turns up for a game with both his ears bandaged up.

"Whatever happened to your ears?" asks the Referee.

The Assistant Referee replies: "Yesterday I was ironing my Referee's top when the phone rang. I accidentally answered with the iron."

"That explains one ear, but whatever happened to the other?" continues the Referee.

"Well, after that I had to call the doctor."

The three English officials were in France for an important UEFA game.

The night before the match the referee had a bit of a sore throat and as a precaution went to the nearby pharmacy. The pharmacist, who spoke some English with a charming Maurice Chevalier accent, explained as he handed over the packet of large capsules :

" We call zeez 'soup-oz- ee-treez'. Verree good for eellness".

The following morning, over breakfast, one of the assistants asked the referee whether he managed to get anything for his throat and how he was feeling.

"Yes, I did get some capsules from the chemist but, to be honest, for all the good they've done me, I might just as well have stuck them up my backside".

What has an IQ of 100?

A 100 referees.

What do you do when you show an angry six-foot tall, thick-set player the red card?

Stand well out of reach.

What is football?

A game played with an inflated ball, twenty two players, two linesmen and several thousand referees.

The referee was invited to officiate at an international tournament in the US. He stayed with an American colleague. The day after the end of the tournament his host suggested a trip to a nearby native American – Red Indian – Reservation, especially to meet the very famous medicine man who had a side-line as a Sports Memory Man.

The referee and his friends were introduced to a small weather-beaten old Indian in traditional dress squatting at the back of the wigwam. After exchanging introductions and pleasantries, the medicine man confirmed that he would answer questions on 'soccer' and indeed on 'refereeing'.

"No problem" he said. "What is first question?"

"Can you tell us who the English referee was who blew his whistle in the World Cup as the ball was about to enter the net, and prevented the winning goal?"

"He called Clive Thomas. He not English referee, he Welsh referee. World Cup 1978 – Brazil v. Sweden. Final score 1-1."

The referee was astonished as well as embarrassed and muttered his thanks and an apology for getting Clive's nationality wrong.

"A second question?"

"Who invented red and yellow cards?"

"Ken Aston, English referee. Famous for trying to control *Battle of Santiago*, Chile v. Italy, World Cup 1962."

He got idea on way home from match. See traffic lights changing, green, yellow, red".

The referee was so amazed he could hardly phrase his final clincher question.

"When did England last win the World Cup"

First and last time – 1966 at Wembley. Beat Germany 4-2. Same year World Cup stolen and found by dog in London.

The stunned visitors thanked the medicine man profusely and made a handsome donation to the Reservation Benevolent Fund.

Some years later, the referee was again delighted to be invited to officiate at the tournament and stayed with the same American friends.

"Why not another visit to the Reservation to see if the medicine man is still doing the business?"

They were assured he was and were taken to his wigwam. As the referee went in he raised his hand to the Memory Man in Indian salute and said:

"How."

"Full time score 2-2; 98th minute Hurst shot bounce down from crossbar, Russian linesman give goal, then Hurst score again with crowd on pitch . .

Argument about game not over yet".

Referee blows for the infringement

Player: "Direct or indirect ref?"

Referee (indicating his arm stretching skywards) : "What do you think this is supposed to mean?"

Player: "Well, if you don't know ref, what bloody chance have we got?"

The referee only officiated on Sundays because he was a keen supporter of the local Football League team. He and his wife had season tickets. The team had got to the quarter final of the FA Cup for the first time for years and the match was a sell-out.

As he took his seat, the referee's neighbour saw that the wife's seat was empty.

"Nice to see you. Your missus coming later?"

"No. I'm, afraid she's passed away".

"Oh I am really sorry to hear that. We'll miss her. She was a really nice lady. Couldn't you get one of the family to take the seat?"

"No, unfortunately I couldn't. They're all at the funeral."

The referee was visited by an American friend, keen, of course, on their sort of 'football', but not very clued up about 'soccer'.

Visitor: "Do the players really just kick the ball around, on grass, out-of-doors, whatever the weather?"

Referee: "Yes, they do."

Visitor: "And you have to run around, blowing your whistle, keeping them in line?"

Referee: "Yes, I do."

Visitor: "When there's snow on the ground, I guess you have red or blue balls."

Referee: "No way. I always wear thermal underpants."

What do you call a referee who goes into the club bar after the home team has lost to a disputed penalty?

A nutter.

What is the difference between a referee and a battery?

The battery has a positive side.

What is a referee's favourite pet?

His guide dog?

The female referee was having a good game in her quietly efficient way. Suddenly one of the home team's strikers broke through just outside the penalty box and was unceremoniously scythed down by the visiting captain.

"OFF! OFF! OFF! OFF! chanted the crowd.

1st fan: "She won't send him off you know. She hasn't got the balls."

2nd fan: "Exactly."

In the TV chat show, the guests were a psychologist and a referee. The host said he wanted to explore the relationship between the spectators and the referee. Why do the fans chant things like: 'The referee's a bastard', and worse?

The psychologist pointed out that such expressions illustrated the alienation the spectator felt from the authority figure interfering in the legitimate belligerence of their champions, symbolising, as they did, traditional tribal warfare. The reference to the referee's doubtful parentage was an intuitive expression indicative of deep-seated prejudice and of profound socio-psychological significance.

"Do you agree?" the host asked his other guest, the referee.

"Oh, I just assumed they didn't like referees."

The referee suspected he was terminally ill and asked his wife to send for the priest.

"Father", he said, "Thanks for coming. I just need to ask what it's like on the other side."

"Wonderful, my son. Now, I know you're a referee and there's good news and bad news. Which would you like to hear first?"

"Give me the good news, father. Prepare me for the bad."

"Well, it really is Heaven for referees. Wonderful grounds, facilities you've never dreamed of, spectators who welcome you and players who apologise if they happen to commit a foul. You'll love it."

"Sounds great. What's the bad news then father?"

"You've got your first game this Saturday."

"My wife informed me last week she'd leave me if I didn't stop spending so much time refereeing football matches.

"That's a rotten shame."

"It is. I'd really miss her."

The defender, always willing to help the referee, shouted: "Come on, ref, offside!" The referee waved play on.

The player was not at all happy and shouted: "You must be bloody blind, ref."

The experienced referee was quite unfazed: "I didn't hear that, no 3."

"Come on, ref. You bloody deaf as well?" was the instant response.

Referees are traditionally alleged to be the product of one-parent families, born with appalling eyesight, and with a knowledge of football that begins and ends with the letter of the law. Well, let me say straight away that that is just not true. It only applies to 99% of them.

A football hooligan appeared in court charged with disorderly conduct and assault. The arresting officer, giving evidence, stated that the accused had thrown something into the canal. "What exactly was it that he threw into the canal?" asked the magistrate.

"Stones, sir."

"Well, that's hardly an offence is it?"

"It was in this case, sir," said the police officer.

"Stones was the referee."

After having a real stinker of a game, the referee said cheerfully to the assessor: "I suppose you've seen worse referees in your time?" There wasn't a flicker of a reply.

"I suppose you've seen worse referees in your time?" the referee repeated louder and more insistently.

"It's all right. I heard you the first time. I'm just trying to remember when."

The ref was a Slav from Treblanka
The assistants both came from Sri Lanka
Though their English was good
What was not understood
Was the fans' favourite cry: 'You're a W****r !

There was a young ref name of Baring,
Who couldn't abide any swearing.
 If a wrong word was said
He would pull out the red
"That'll teach you to be rather less daring!"

The game was becoming quite rough
And the ref felt the need to get tough.
He tried very hard
Not to use the red card,
But the yellow just proved not enough

The young referee had fallen on hard times and liked his mate's suggestion of doing a bit of begging on the Underground for some temporary relief. His friend said it was lucrative, but stressed that you had to find a way to get the public's sympathy.

The man took up his position in one of the main entrance tunnels, sitting with his back against the wall, wearing dark glasses, with a white stick beside him and a notice round his neck bearing the words:

BLIND, MENTALLY HANDICAPPED, AND NO FATHER.

The first passer-by hesitated, dropped a £1 coin into the hat and leaned over confidentially:

"Excuse me sir. Are you by any chance a football referee?"

The astonished beggar replied: "As is happens I am. But however did you know?"

"Well, those are the problems they all have" the passer-by replied sympathetically.

The referee arrived at the Pearly Gates and was met by the angel in charge.

"Welcome, my son. Before you can enter Heaven I need to ask whether there is anything you would want to confess."

"Well," said the referee in some embarrassment, "I suppose I should admit one thing. In an international I was refereeing between Scotland and Wales, I gave a penalty for Wales that won them the game. I saw the replay afterwards and I don't think the Scottish defender ever touched the ball with his hand. It's been on my conscience ever since."

"You don't need to worry my son. You certainly made the correct decision."

"Oh thank you St Peter," said the referee. "That's a real load off my mind."

"By the way," said the angel, "It's St Peter's day off. I'm St David."

The doctor wasn't sure about the rash on the referee's arm and decided he should have a second opinion. The consultant dermatologist was not unhappy and decided a normal steroid cream would soon clear the problem up. As he was finishing writing his notes, he looked up and said:

"By the way, are you by any chance a football referee?"

"As it happens I am. But however did you know?"

"Well, your's is the thickest skin I've ever come across."

When the case for professional referees was being discussed, it was announced that the Premiership was going to ask FIFA for permission for them to have a sponsor's logo on their shirts to help defray the cost. The RNIB was suggested.

Footballer to team doctor : I'm really worried. Something's gone wrong with my eyes. I can't see very well and things seem to be coloured red and yellow

Doctor : No problem. You should just train to be a referee.

It was the Annual Charity match between a team made up of doctors and one chosen from the rest of the hospital staff.

When one of the doctor defenders fouled an opponent in the box, the (neutral) referee immediately indicated the penalty.

"Hold on ref", shouted a defender colleague, "you must be bloody blind".

The experienced official, hoping to keep things low-key as it was a charity match, kept his card in his pocket and retorted:

"When I want your opinion no 3, I'll ask for it"

"And I'll charge you 50 quid", was the instant quip from the ophthalmic consultant.

Small boy : "Mu-um".

Mother : "Yes, Darren".

Small boy : "Teacher says I have to see the Schools' sikia - something".

Mother : "Who? Did she say *Psychiatrist?*"

Small boy : "I think so"

Mother, anxiously : "Did she say why? What had you been doing?"

Small boy : "Nothing Mum, honest. She just asked what we wanted to be when we grew up and all I said was: "A referee like my dad."

It was a fair decision the penalty, even though it was debatable whether it was outside or inside the box.

Bobby Charlton

The referee was booking everyone. I thought he was filling in his lottery numbers.

Ian Wright

Watching their local team in action, the fan remarked to his referee friend :

I see their manager's reffing today. He looks a real novice."

"He certainly is. When I asked him if he used the diagonal method of control, he asked me if I was a sex therapist."

The referee was surprised to be asked by the local zoo to take charge of a match between a team of mammals and a team of insects. By half-time the mammals were leading comfortably 10-0.

However, at half-time the insects made a substitution and brought on a centipede. By the end he had scored no fewer than 27 goals and the insects won a famous victory : 27-10.

As they left the field, the referee, overcome by curiosity, approached the insect captain. "That centipede of yours was brilliant. But why didn't you play him from the start?"

"We'd have liked to," was the reply "but it takes him the first 45 minutes to get his boots on."

My reasons for becoming a referee

I love football but never could understand it.

I am visually challenged and uncertain of my parentage.

I love to run around a football field, not allowed to kick the ball, in the cold, wind and rain.

I love to be abused and physically threatened.

I have the knack of always being able to make the wrong decision.

One day Jesus confided to St Peter that he fancied a game of football. As He was clearly set on the project, Peter, who acted as minder on these occasions, said he would accompany Him to Earth.

The local country league game was about to start, so Jesus assumed the persona of the right midfielder and Peter settled to be the referee, so that he could be best placed to keep an eye on things.

The keeper collected the ball and threw it out to Jesus near his right touch line. Jesus neatly beat two men then hit a long diagonal pass for his left side attacker way forward near the far touch line. The ball went like a rocket, high and handsome, way beyond its destination and with one bounce ended up in the middle of the village pond. Without hesitation Jesus sprinted the hundred yards or so and walked across the water to retrieve it.

As He ran back to hand it to the opponent for the throw-in, the astonished visiting captain said to the referee (St Peter) "Did you see that? Who does he think he is? Jesus Christ?"

Sadly St Peter replied. "No, that's just the trouble. He doesn't. He thinks He's David Beckham."

The recently retired Premiership and FIFA referee was into good works.

At the old peoples' home he said to a very elderly man watching football on the TV :
"I see you're interested in football"

"I certainly am", was the firm reply. "Been an Arsenal supporter for over 80 years."

"Great." replied the referee enthusiastically. "Do you know who I am?"

"No, but if you ask her nicely, Matron will be happy to tell you".

There is no truth in the rumour that the renowned Italian referee Pierluigi Collina had his hair cut so short because he has eyes in the back of his head and couldn't stand having his vision obstructed.

"I just don't understand it," the referee said to his assessor:

"One match I do very well, then the next match I'm terrible. And that's what you saw today."

"Well," said the assessor helpfully, "maybe you should just do every other game."

A well-known referee was called as a character witness in a matrimonial case and, on being asked his profession, replied :

"I am the greatest referee in the world."

After the case was over, he came in for a good deal of ribbing from his referee colleagues.

"How could you possibly stand up in court and say a thing like that?" they asked.

"Well," he replied: "you must remember I was under oath!"

The ref was vertically 15 yards away.

Kevin Keegan

I think you and the referee were in a minority of one, Billy.

Jimmy Armfield

The tall, six-footed, tanned referee from Spain . . .

John Clayton

The referee's wife was convinced her husband was obsessive about football and about his refereeing in particular and she finally persuaded him to get professional help. For a quiet life the husband agreed. The famous psychiatrist's method was to show his patients letters of the alphabet. From their reaction, he claimed, he could detect any psychological abnormalities.

He welcomed the referee and emphasised that he wanted him to react *immediately* to the card shown to him.

The psychiatrist showed him the letter 'X'.
"A penalty mark."

The letter 'd'.
"A referee signaling an indirect free kick."

The letter 'o'.
"A football."

The letter 'I'.
"A corner flag."

The psychiatrist carefully stacked his letter cards and looked gravely at his patient.

"I'm afraid your wife is absolutely right. You do have a deep-seated obsession with football and refereeing."

Referee : "What do you mean, *I* have an obsession? *You* chose the bloody cards."

The Sunday League 4th Division game didn't get an appointed referee, so the home team manager stood in.

He wasn't doing badly until one of his own team committed a horrendous tackle. After a fierce blast of the whistle, he motioned the guilty player over and tore him off a strip. His notebook stayed in his pocket but he concluded by saying very loudly:

"And if anything like that happens again, you're off!"

The chastised player looked up sheepishly and muttered: "Thanks Dad."

Question from first fan:

"What do you do if you find a referee buried up to his neck in sand?"

Answer from second fan:

"Get more sand."

As the referee called the captains over before the start of the game, he noticed a large red-setter dog in full kit with the Red team.

"Nice dog. Somebody's mascot?" he enquired of the Reds with a smile.

"No ref, he's playing for us," replied the Reds' captain.

Suspecting some kind of joke, the referee looked more closely and saw that the dog was indeed not only in full kit, but even had specially made shinguards. And there were certainly only ten other players

"He's registered and he's on the team sheet" the captain went on helpfully, and the referee remembered he had noticed the unusual first name 'Ared Setter'

"It's all right, ref, they don't ask you whether you're a dog when you register. And, before you ask, he talks as well."

By now the referee is really concerned. He's sure there's something funny going on but he can't think of any reason in the Laws or the Competition Rules that would allow him to say no to the dog.

80

"Right lads, off we go then."

For about ten minutes the ball doesn't go near the dog playing in midfield. Then a clearance out of the opposition's defence is going to drop near him. .

With a spectacular leap the dog heads the ball down and controls it with his back legs under his body. With an astonishing turn of speed and a fantastic body swerve the dog evades all the attempted tackles as he makes the 60 yards into the opposition's penalty area. Then he lets fly a powerful shot, right into the top corner of the net.

Whistle goes but, when the dog turns with his shirt half off in celebration, he sees the referee pointing to the ground near his feet.

"Defence free kick".

"No way, ref", protested the dog. "That was a bloody good goal."

"Sorry mate," said the referee with the hint of a satisfied smile. "You shot with one of your front paws. So it had to be handball !"

Near the end of a tense cup-tie with the score at 1-1, one of the players flagrantly held an opponent back when he was about to shoot for goal. The victim was about to pole-axe his assailant when the referee skilfully intervened.

"Now you know you'll be off if you retaliate, O'Hara."

"Aw, come on ref. He retaliated first."

The referee was surprised to be pressed to take an Under 11 game 'because it would be a needle match'.

When the first half passed without incident and the score was 10 – 0, he really did wonder whether his journey had been worthwhile.

However . . . As he walked over to the losing team to call them for the re-start, he heard the young captain energetically rallying his troops:

"Come on lads. Give it all you've got. We're letting this one slip away."

A senior English referee was delighted to be appointed to his first international middle in Russia.

The evening before the match was free, so he decided to take a short walk. He was enjoying a drink in a small bar when a very attractive local girl came and sat down opposite him.

'Hello,' he said, 'Do you understand English?'

'Only a leetle bit,' replied the girl.

'But how much?' asked the referee.

'I start at twentee Eengleesh pounds,' she replied

After a pathetic performance, the new referee was approached by one of the spectators.

"Didn't go too well today ref. I think I may be able to help you."

"Oh, you a referee trainer then?"

"No, I'm an optician."

There is no truth in the rumour that many referees are now suffering from RSI (Repetitive Strain Injury) because of the frequency of arm-raising to show red and yellow cards.

The condition is also known as FAD (Functional Arthritic Disorder) or, as the fans prefer, F****** Awful Decisions.

During a Diadora League match Bognor's Paul Pullen voiced his unhappiness with one of the referee's decisions, having already been cautioned. To his surprise, the referee called over his twin brother, Mick, and sent him off despite the player's protests of innocence.

A player down-under who allegedly backhanded the referee was offered an unusual deal by the judicial committee – either to have a one-year ban or *to become a referee for a year.*

In his pre-match chat with his assistants, the referee was stressing to his assistants the importance of showing respect for the players and establishing communication. He opened the home team's changing room door and called "Gentlemen".

That raised the first laugh.

"I am Joseph Bloggs, schoolmaster, your referee for the day, and these are my assistants : Henry Brown, who is a sales manager, and Jonathan Green, a car mechanic.

At the end of a lengthy talk explaining his approach to the game in great detail, Mr Bloggs asked if any of the players had a question.

"Yes" was the instant reply from one of them looking straight at Mr Green, the car mechanic. "It's just that I've got this problem with the wife's *Yaris . . . ."*

"We're starting an amateur football team. Would you like to join?"

"Yes I would, but I don't know the first thing about football."

"Oh, that's all right. We need a referee as well."

The GP rang his consultant psychiatrist friend with an urgent request.

"Hello James. I would like you to see a patient of mine as soon as possible."

"Right, John. Who is it?"

"He's a well-known football referee."

"Ah, ah. Has he any other suicidal tendencies?"

The referee was telling his newly qualified colleague about a player he had had to send off in a recent match.

"His problem is he's temperamental."

"How do you mean 'temperamental'"?

"50% temper and 50% mental."

The 1878 Cup Final between Wanderers and Royal Engineers was refereed by a Mr S.R. Bastard

A match between Coventry City and Southend United had been in progress for three full minutes before anyone, including referee Arthur Holland, noticed that both teams were playing in blue and white.

Total Football teamed up with Vision Express, the national optician chain, to offer cut-price eye tests for referees.

The tables were turned on referee David Elleray at Leeds when the players complained of a colour clash between his black uniform and the Newcastle United strip. Elleray dutifully changed into a borrowed blue Leeds United T-shirt.

The referee met his fellow referee during the week.

First referee: "How did it go last weekend?"

Second referee: "Terrible. I had a real nightmare. Difficulty parking the car, huge crowd. I got jostled and treated with no respect at all. It was very physical and demanding, and I had to use the card several times.

I'm never going shopping with my wife again on a Saturday."

The referee was in hospital recovering
from a serious bout of pneumonia. As
one of his nurses was collecting his
breakfast tray, she said confidentially :

"Excuse me, sir. Are you by any chance a
football referee?"

 "As it happens I am. But why do you
ask?"

"It's just that when you were delirious,
you kept muttering:

 *"I know both my parents .. I know
both my parents."*

One night three referees had a similar dream. God thanked them for what they were doing to help people to enjoy their football and, as a reward, he would answer any question they asked about their refereeing.

The first referee said: "Can you tell me when I will get a local cup final middle?"

"In five years' time" God replied. "I'll have retired by then" said the referee.

The second one asked: "Can you tell me when I will get a County Cup final middle?"

Yes, in ten years' time" was the reply. "I'll have retired by then" said the second referee.

The third one asked: "Can you tell me when I will get the FA Cup final middle?

God replied: "*I'll* have retired by then."

What is the difference between a man awaiting a hospital operation and a referee?

The patient is _on_ his trolley.

The attacking no 8 was barely touched in the penalty box but dramatically flew head-over-heals. The referee was not conned. He whistled and strode purposefully towards the prostrate player already loudly claiming a penalty.

"Now number 8, what do you call that?"

Opposition goalkeeper, helpfully: "Double forward somersault with pike?"

Trainee referee: "What do you do if someone calls you a b*****d?"

Instructor: "No problem. Offensive language, red card and send him off."

Trainee referee: "But what do you do if it's true?"

Father and son were watching a football match.

"Dad. Why do you keep calling the referee a 'Potter'? Is it because he's a wizard like Harry?"

"No way. It's because he's a real Pansy."

The referee's wife was watching him carefully preparing his kit for his next game. "That's all you ever think about. You never think about me or us. I bet you can't even remember when we got married."

"Oh yes, I can," her husband retorted triumphantly, "it was the day before I had that Senior Cup Final in 1990 and gave a brilliant penalty decision in the last minute that decided the match."

If Mickey Mouse had taken charge it would have given the place a lift.

Mike Walker

I have nothing against the visually handicapped as such, but I am just surprised they are allowed to referee at this level.

Anon

Mother to Father: "I think our son has the makings of a football hooligan. Last week he called the referee a 'right W*****' and today he threw a bottle.

I don't care what he thinks about referees – we all think the same - but you really must do something about him. This time he smashed the TV screen . . ."

The referee was careful to have an eye test every two years.

He was sitting in the chair awaiting his tests when the optometrist said: "Excuse me sir, are you by any chance a referee? The referee admitted he was.

Optometrist: "Wasn't it you in charge of the ManU home game that was on TV last Saturday?" The referee agreed he was.

Without further comment the optometrist took the referee through the full series of tests.

Optometrist: "Well, sir, you have really excellent vision."

The referee smiled, unable to conceal his satisfaction

Optometrist: "So how do you explain your abysmal performance at Old Trafford last Saturday?"

Man who see nothing and get everything right, he football manager.

Man who see everything and get nothing right, he football referee.

The novice Assistant Referee was having a torrid time:

"Get yer flag up, Lino!" "Get yer flag down, Lino!" "Get yer eyes tested, Lino!"

At last he could stand it no longer. He turned and shouted at his tormentors: "Why do you keep calling me Lino?"

"Cos you'd be much better at home laid out on the floor!"

Taking out his yellow card, the Sunday League referee strode purposefully towards the rather overweight defender:

"Caution number 3, that tackle was late."

"Aw, come on, ref, I got there as fast as I could !"

That ref today could certainly have done with eyes in the back of his head – he didn't seem to have any at the front.

Anon

The referee's generally had a good game and only put a few feet wrong.

Ray Wilkins

Not one Millwall player surrounded the referee.

David Pleat

I would also think the action replay showed it to be worse than it actually was.

Anon

Player: "What would you do,
             ref, if I called you a
             f****** w*****?"

Referee: "Red card and straight
             off!

Player: "What would you do if I
             thought you were a
             f****** w*****?"

Referee: "You can *think*
             whatever you like."

Player: "In that case, I *think*
             you're a f******
             w*****!"

The new referee had learned that success as an official was all about building up a good rapport with the players. So, after a particularly nasty foul, he approached the player calmly and spoke without raising his voice.

Referee: "Now, did you or did you not kick the number 7?"

Player: "I did and I didn't."

Referee (bemused): 'What do you mean *you did and you didn't*?'

Player: "Well, I *did* kick him but I *didn't* think you'd be quick enough to spot it!"

Referee to assessor: "You don't think I'm big-headed about my refereeing do you?"

Assessor: "Oh,why do you ask?"

Referee: "It's just that referees as good as me usually are."

In a European Cup match, the English striker was flattened by a German defender in the area. He appealed to the French referee in no uncertain terms for a penalty

In his heavy music hall accent the referee, proud of his grasp of the English tongue, explained:

"No way, monsieur. You sink I know nussing. Let me tell you, monsieur - about football an' refereeing an' penalties, I know bugger all."

Before the Assistant Referee put on his kit he dusted himself liberally with talcum powder, so the first time he broke into a sprint, a huge puff of talc issued from his shorts.

Instant shout from the crowd:

"Look out, Lino, yer balls are on fire."

After being barracked for most of the game, the referee finally cracked and shouted at his principal tormentor:

"Who's refereeing this game? You or me?"

"Neither of us" was the instant reply.

Referee Ivan Robinson inadvertently resolved the stalemate when Barrow and Plymouth were playing out a goalless draw. He couldn't get out of the way of a firmly-struck shot by a Barrow forward that was going well wide and deflected it neatly into the goal.

It is reported that he did not stay behind for a drink at the end of the game.

The referee was back in the
dressing room after the game
which hadn't gone as well as he'd
hoped. Knock on the door and the
assessor walked in

The referee smiled: "How did I
do?"

The assessor hesitated only a
moment:

 "I've seen a really wonderful
refereeing performance. . . . ."

The referee beamed with relief and
pleasure.

"But that certainly wasn't it."

The man arrives at the Pearly Gates and is stopped by God.

"I understand you were a referee in your earthly life, my son."

"I was, Holy Father."

"Did you always try to make fair decisions?"

"I did, Holy Father."

Is there anything you want to confess to me about your life as a referee?"

"There is, Holy Father."

"And what is that, my son?"

"When I was refereeing an international in South America I gave a doubtful penalty against the home team."

"And when was that, my son?"

"About three minutes ago, Holy Father."

The referee had accidentally collided with a player, fallen and injured his knee.

On his way back from the doctor's surgery after the match, he met one of the players from the game.

"You all right ref? You don't look so good. Bad news from the doc?"

"Yes it is. He says I can't referee."

"Oh. Seen you in action has he . . .?"

Norman Hunter was notorious for his 'robust' tackles. After a particularly doubtful challenge, the referee who knew him well, called him over and said firmly :

"Too much that time, Norman. Got to be a caution."

"Aw, come on, ref. You've forgotten I was the one who went home last season with a broken leg."

Referee: "Whose?"

The Devil, who was a keen football fan, decided to challenge Heaven to a friendly game.

St Peter was delighted to be asked but, a strong believer in fair play, he was worried that the match would be too one-sided as he had all the best players. He so replied to the Devil who burst into laughter.

"I know what you're thinking, but you've forgotten something vital - I've got all the referees !"

A referee is someone who likes to be out in the cold, the heat, the wet. To be shouted at, insulted, physically threatened and mad enough to be looking forward to next week's game . .

There is no truth in the rumour that referees run the diagonals because they are all cross-eyed.

Sir Alex Ferguson had gone for a picnic with Ryan Giggs and Premiership referee. Howard Webb. They spread the groundsheet on the bank of a river across from a country pub.

"I'll get the first round" said Giggs, walked straight across the river and returned the same way, carrying the tray of brimming glasses. Sir Alex was astonished but said nothing.

They were nicely into the sandwiches when Howard Webb announced "The next one's on me" picked up the tray, walked across the river and returned with the drinks. Sir Alex could hardly contain himself but still kept silent.

At the end of the meal, with the glasses once more empty, Sir Alex stood and said "Right lads, my shout."

With a look of panic, Giggs turned to Howard Webb and said in an urgent whisper "Shouldn't we tell him about the concealed stepping stones?"

"What stepping stones?" asked Howard Webb.

The referee trainer believed in starting by getting the basics right. Picking up a football, he said:

"Right, lads, what I have in my hands is called a *football*, and the object of the game is . . . ."

"Hang on a minute," came a shout from one of the new trainees, "you're going too fast."

A well-known referee was talking to a football manager at a party.

"I've been persuaded to write my autobiography," he said, "but I don't want it published until after I'm dead."

"Really?" said the manager. "I shall look forward to reading it."

At the primary school sports day, parents were encouraged to take part in the 50yd dash. The referee was pressed by his wife into entering 'for the sake of the children'. As he walked away afterwards, he was approached by the head teacher.

"Excuse me, sir. Are you by any chance a football referee?"

"As it happens I am. But however did you know?"

"Well, you were the only parent who ran the whole race backwards with his arm up in the air."

The referee had gone to see his doctor because he was getting breathless towards the end of games. The doctor examined him thoroughly and pronounced:

"You're generally fit but, to put it simply, you're too fat."

"What do you mean, 'I'm too fat'? I'd like to have a second opinion."

"OK. You're a lousy referee as well."

When the referee was at the supermarket till, the cashier surprised him by asking:

"Excuse me, sir, are you by any chance a football referee?"

"Yes I am, but how did you know?

"It's just that you are trying to pay with a yellow card".

The experienced English FIFA referee was giving a few tips to his newly promoted colleague who was worried about his ignorance of the local language.

"No problem. You'll cope perfectly well with your whistle, two cards and . . . *Any more and you're off !*"

The Football League referee had shown one red and seven yellow cards in the match and so was making a quiet exit from the ground.

When he got to his car, he discovered it was blocked in by the visiting team's coach. He very reluctantly went back to the dressing room and called out: "Does anyone know where your coach driver is?"

"Who ref? Our coach driver? You going to book him as well?"

It's like a toaster the ref's shirt pocket. Every time there's a tackle, up pops a yellow card.

Kevin Keegan

Of the nine red cards this season, we probably deserved half of them.

Arsène Wenger

The player had been summoned to the referee after a particularly nasty foul. As the referee took out his book for the third time that afternoon, the player could be seen mouthing a response.

First commentator: "It looks as if he's telling the referee where to put the card."

Second commentator: "That won't do him any good. There are two cards up there already."

Clearly a body check and a yellow card was certainly merited. Calling the player over the referee said politely :

"Your name please".

"Bugger off" was the immediate reply.

Just as he was reaching for his *red* card the referee remembered the club's new signing from one of the former Soviet republics – Yevgeni Bugarov

Whether that was a penalty or not, the referee thought otherwise.

John Motson

I never comment on referees and I'm not going to break the habit of a life-time for that prat.

Ron Atkinson

129

The referee just didn't seem able to get anything right.

One agitated spectator was turning to his neighbour to make a suitably colourful remark, when the referee started to gesticulate and shouted :

"ADVANTAGE !"

"So that's his problem. He thinks he's reffing a bloody game of tennis!"

Cartoon by Clip Project (www.clipproject.info)

20156446R00077

Printed in Poland
by Amazon Fulfillment
Poland Sp. z o.o., Wrocław